P9-DXH-838

D0037780

America Is Not
All Traffic Lights

America Is Not All Traffic Lights

POEMS OF THE MIDWEST

Selected by Alice Fleming

Illustrated with Photographs

Little, Brown and Company   BOSTON   TORONTO

FIRST EDITION

T 02/76

Library of Congress Cataloging in Publication Data

Main entry under title:

America is not all traffic lights.

    SUMMARY: An anthology of poems reflecting the
ambience of the Midwest through such voices as
William Rose Benét, Carl Sandburg, and Sherwood
Anderson.
    1. Middle West—Description and travel—Juvenile
poetry. 2. Poetry of places—Middle West.
[1. Middle West—Poetry. 2. Poetry of places—
Middle West. 3. American poetry—Collections]
I. Fleming, Alice Mulcahey, 1928–
PN6110.P7M5   811'.008'032   75-25651
ISBN 0–316–28590–0

*Published simultaneously in Canada
by Little, Brown & Company (Canada) Limited*

PRINTED IN THE UNITED STATES OF AMERICA

The photographs on pages 2, 6, 8, 22, 26, 30, 34, 38, 40, 44, 54, and 58 appear courtesy of the
Library of Congress.

The photograph on page 18 appears courtesy of the National Park Service.

The photograph on page 26 appears courtesy of the Erwin E. Smith Collection of Range-life
Photographs, Library of Congress.

The photograph on page 62 appears courtesy of The Bettman Archive.

Mrs. Fleming wishes to thank the following for permission to use their poems in this anthology:

"Crossing Kansas by Train" by Donald Justice. Copyright © 1963 by Donald Justice. Reprinted from *Night Light,* by Donald Justice, by permission of Wesleyan University Press. This poem first appeared in *The New Yorker.*

"Lucas Park (St. Louis)" by Paul Southworth Bliss from *Poems of Places* by Paul Southworth Bliss, the Cirrus Company, Bismarck. Copyright 1937 by Paul Southworth Bliss.

"Illinois Farmer" from *Cornhuskers* by Carl Sandburg, copyright 1918, by Holt, Rinehart and Winston, Inc., copyright 1946, by Carl Sandburg. Reprinted by permission of Harcourt Brace Jovanovich, Inc.

"Jesse James" by William Rose Benét, from *Man Possessed.* Copyright 1927 by William Rose Benét. Renewed. Reprinted by permission of Harold Ober Associates Incorporated.

"Chicago/3 Hours" by Victor Hernandez Cruz. From *Mainland* by Victor Hernandez Cruz. Copyright © 1973 by Victor Hernandez Cruz. Reprinted by permission of Random House, Inc.

"Midwest" by John Frederick Nims. Reprinted by permission of William Morrow and Co., Inc. from *The Iron Pastoral* by John Frederick Nims. Copyright 1947 by John Frederick Nims.

"La Salle Street" by Rachel Albright, from *Poems of the Middle West* by Rachel Albright, The Torch Press, Cedar Rapids, Iowa, 1942.

"Part of the Darkness" by Isabella Gardner from *The Looking Glass* by Isabella Gardner. Copyright © 1961 by the University of Chicago Press.

"Midwest Town" by Ruth De Long Peterson, from "The Beauty of America," reprinted from *Saturday Evening Post.* Copyright © 1954 by Ruth De Long Peterson. Reprinted by permission of the author.

"Evening Song" by Sherwood Anderson from *Mid-American Chants* by Sherwood Anderson. Reprinted by permission of Harold Ober Associates Incorporated. Copyright 1918 by John Lane Company. Renewed 1945 by Eleanor Copenhaver Anderson.

"July in Indiana" by Robert Fitzgerald from *Spring Shade.* Copyright © 1966 by Robert Fitzgerald. "July in Indiana" was first published in *The New Yorker.* Reprinted by permission of New Directions Publishing Corporation.

"A Blessing" by James Wright. Copyright © 1961 by James Wright. Reprinted from *Collected Poems* by James Wright, by permission of Wesleyan University Press. "A Blessing" first appeared in *Poetry.*

"Finale" by Carl Sandburg. From "Prairie" in *Cornhuskers* by Carl Sandburg. Reprinted by permission of Harcourt Brace Jovanovich, Inc.

Osage Chant from "The Osage Tribe, Part II" *The Rite of Vigil,* translated by Dr. Francis La Flesche, 39th Annual Report. Bureau of American Ethnology, Washington, D.C. 1925, pp. 31–630.

"Of De Witt Williams on His Way To Lincoln Cemetery" from *The World of Gwendolyn Brooks* (1971) by Gwendolyn Brooks. Copyright 1945 by Gwendolyn Brooks Blakely. Reprinted by permission of Harper & Row, Publishers Inc.

Contents

Foreword

The poems in this book present a view of the Midwest that goes beyond the descriptions in a travel guide or the pictures in a geography book. They were chosen because they capture, in graceful language and vivid images, the sights and sounds, moods and memories of America's heartland.

The Midwest has produced or inspired an impressive number of poets. This book contains just a few of the hundreds of poems they have written. But these few offer a unique insight into what Middle America means to those who see it with a poet's vision and can describe it with a poet's gifts.

Alice Fleming

America Is Not
All Traffic Lights

Crossing Kansas by Train

The telephone poles
have been holding their
arms out
a long time now
to birds
that will not settle there
but pass with
strange cawings
westward to
where dark trees
gather about
a waterhole. This
is Kansas. The
mountains start here
just behind
the closed eyes
of a farmer's
sons asleep
in their workclothes.

Donald Justice

Lucas Park (St. Louis)

Old men
In Lucas Park,
Sitting respectfully
About a fountain,
Half hearing,
Half seeing,
Half feeling,
Amidst the cannas,
And the coleus;
Old men,
Sitting like mummers
At a funeral . . .

Old men,
Spreading newspapers,
Bedding down for the night;
Old men,
Like figures
In a charade of death;

Old men,
Sleeping
Under a sanctimonious moon;
Old men,
like corpses
On mortuary slabs . . .

Old men,
Shivering at dawn;
Old men,
Moving off stiffly
To comfort stations
And a plate of Dempsey soup;
Old men,
In Lucas Park,
Keeping off the grass,
Sitting quietly
About the fountain,
Amidst the santolina,
And the echevira
And the century plants.

Paul Southworth Bliss

Illinois Farmer

Bury this old Illinois farmer with respect.
He slept the Illinois nights of his life after days of work in
       Illinois cornfields.
Now he goes on a long sleep.
The wind he listened to in the cornsilk and the tassels, the
       wind that combed his red beard zero mornings when the
       snow lay white on the yellow ears in the bushel basket
       at the corncrib,
The same wind will now blow over the place here where his
       hands must dream of Illinois corn.

Carl Sandburg

Jesse James

A Design in Red and Yellow for a Nickel Library

Jesse James was a two-gun man,
  (*Roll on, Missouri!*)
Strong-arm chief of an outlaw clan,
  (*From Kansas to Illinois!*)
He twirled an old Colt forty-five;
  (*Roll on, Missouri!*)
They never took Jesse James alive.
  (*Roll, Missouri, roll!*)

Jesse James was King of the Wes';
  (*Cataracts in the Missouri!*)
He'd a di'mon' heart in his lef' breas';
  (*Brown Missouri rolls!*)
He'd a fire in his heart no hurt could stifle,
  (*Thunder, Missouri!*)
Lion eyes an' a Winchester rifle.
  (*Missouri, roll down!*)

Jesse James rode a pinto hawse;
Come at night to a water-cawse;
Tetched with the rowel that pinto's flank;
She sprung the torrent from bank to bank.

Jesse rode through a sleepin' town;
Looked the moonlit street both up an' down;
Crack-crack-crack, the street ran flames
An' a great voice cried, "I'm Jesse James!"

Hawse, an' afoot they're after Jess!
    (*Roll on, Missouri!*)
Spurrin' an' spurrin' — but he's gone Wes'.
    (*Brown Missouri rolls!*)
He was ten foot tall when he stood in his boots;
    (*Lightnin' like the Missouri!*)
More 'n a match fer sich galoots.
    (*Roll, Missouri, roll!*)

Jesse James rode outa the sage;
Roun' the rocks come the swayin' stage;
Straddlin' the road a giant stan's
An' a great voice bellers, "Throw up yer han's!"
Jesse raked in the di'mon' rings,
The big gold watches an' the yuther things;
Jesse divvied 'em then an' thar
With a cryin' child had lost her mar.

They're creepin'; they're crawlin'; they're stalkin' Jess;
  (*Roll on, Missouri!*)
They's a rumor he's gone much further Wes';
  (*Roll, Missouri, roll!*)
They's word of a cayuse hitched to the bars
  (*Ruddy clouds on Missouri!*)
Of a golden sunset that busts into stars.
  (*Missouri, roll down!*)

Jesse James rode hell fer leather;
He was a hawse an' a man together;
In a cave in a mountain high up in air
He lived with a rattlesnake, a wolf, an' a bear.

Jesse's heart was as sof' as a woman;
Fer guts an' stren'th he was sooper-human;
He could put six shots through a woodpecker's eye
And take in one swaller a gallon o' rye.

They sought him here an' they sought him there,
  (*Roll on, Missouri*)
But he strides by night through the ways of the air;
  (*Brown Missouri rolls!*)
They say he was took an' they say he is dead,
  (*Thunder, Missouri!*)
But he ain't — he's a sunset overhead!
  (*Missouri down to the sea!*)

Jesse James was a Hercules.
When he went through the woods he tore up the trees.
When he went on the plains he smoked the groun'
An' the hull lan' shuddered fer miles aroun'.

Jesse James wore a red bandanner
That waved on the breeze like the Star Spangled Banner;
In seven states he cut up dadoes.
He's gone with the buffler an' the desperadoes.

Yes, Jesse James was a two-gun man
          (*Roll on, Missouri!*)
The same as when this song began;
          (*From Kansas to Illinois!*)
An' when you see a sunset bust into flames
          (*Lightnin' like the Missouri!*)
Or a thunderstorm blaze — that's Jesse James!
          (*Hear that Missouri roll!*)

                              William Rose Benét

Chicago/ 3 Hours

State Street's cold mingling
crowds of Christmas
The town of garages and lonely
alleys
Traffic chaos —
That melody of a fast moving
civilization
Part cowboy   Part Anglo
for the famous breeze
Bacardi light
Chicago the first apple
for a long long time
Night and theater lights
Night and the river shows waves

A spirit walks the bridge with
cement still tied to his legs
Smoke is wind/ in the wind
Someone told me el hijo de Cortijo
is somewhere in this town
Ay le lo li le lo li
That's enough to keep you warm
Say it one more time
Ay le lo li le lo li.

Victor Hernandez Cruz

Midwest

Indiana: no blustering summit or coarse gorge;
No flora lurid as disaster-flares;
No great vacuities where tourists gape
Nor mountains hoarding their height like millionaires.
More delicate: the ten-foot knolls
Give flavor of hill to Indiana souls.

Topography is perfect, curio-size;
Deft as landscape in museum cases.
What is beautiful is friendly and underfoot,
Not flaunted like theater curtains in our faces.
No peak or jungle obscures the blue sky;
Our land rides smoothly in the softest eye.

Man is the prominent fauna of our state.
Elsewhere circus creatures stomp and leer
With heads like crags or clumps. But delirious nature
Once in a lucid interval sobering here
Left (repenting her extravagant plan)
Conspicuous on our fields the shadow of man.

John Frederick Nims

LaSalle Street

No cedar dares a roothold in the stone
That constitutes these proud gray canyon walls;
This is a metal realm; no linnet calls
Above the armored cars; the robot drone
Of dictaphones personifies this street;
And shadows that obscure your fields are made.
Tall corn of Iowa and Kansas wheat,
By faceless Ceres and the Board of Trade.

The sod holds fee to Cavelier LaSalle;
Alleviate, slim spires, your silver sheen;
A planter trembles in the far Transvaal
And beads are muttered in the Argentine.
New ticker tape curls alabaster white
And men are lonely — each an anchorite.

Rachel Albright

Part of the Darkness

I had thought of the bear in his lair as fiercely free,
    feasting on honey and wildwood fruits;
I had imagined a forest lunge, regretting the circus
    shuffle and the zoo's proscribed pursuits.
Last summer I took books and children to Wisconsin's
    Great North woods. We drove
one night through miles of pine and rainy darkness to
    a garbage grove
that burgeoned broken crates and bulging paper bags
    and emptied cans of beer,
to watch for native bears, who local guides had told us,
    scavenged there.
After parking behind three other cars (leaving our head-
    lights on but dim)
we stumbled over soggy moss to join the families blink-
    ing on the rim
of mounded refuse bounded east north and west by the
    forest.
The parents hushed and warned their pushing children
    each of whom struggled to stand nearest

the arena, and presently part of the darkness humped
    away from the foliage and lumbered bear-shaped
toward the heaping spoilage. It trundled into the litter
    while we gaped,
and for an instant it gaped too, bear-faced, but not a
    tooth was bared. It grovelled
carefully while tin cans clattered and tense tourists tit-
    tered. Painstakingly it nosed and ravelled
rinds and husks and parings, the used and the refused;
    bear-skinned and doggedly explored
the second-hand remains while headlights glared and
    flashlights stared and shamed bored
children booed, wishing aloud that it would trudge away
    so they might read its tracks.
They hoped to find an as yet unclassified spoor, certain
    that no authentic bear would turn his back
upon the delicacies of his own domain to flounder where
    mere housewives' leavings rot.
I also was reluctant to concede that there is no wild
    honey in the forest and no forest in the bear.
Bereaved, we started home, leaving that animal there.

                                        Isabella Gardner

Midwest Town

Farther east it wouldn't be on the map —
　　Too small — but here it rates a dot and name.
In Europe it would wear a castle cap
　　Or have a cathedral rising like a flame.

But here it stands where the section roadways meet,
　　Its houses dignified with trees and lawn;
The stores hold tête-à-tête across Main Street;
　　The red brick school, a church — the town is gone.

America is not all traffic lights
　　And beehive homes and shops and factories;
No, there are wide green days and starry nights,
　　And a great pulse beating strong in towns like these.

Ruth De Long Peterson

Evening Song

Back of Chicago the open fields — were you ever
   there?
Trains coming toward you out of the West —
Streaks of light on the long grey plains?
   Many a song —
Aching to sing.

I've got a grey and ragged brother in my
   breast —
That's a fact.

Back of Chicago the open fields — were you ever
   there?
Trains going from you into the West —
Clouds of dust on the long grey plains.
Long trains go West, too — in the silence.
Always the song —
Waiting to sing.

Sherwood Anderson

July in Indiana

The wispy cuttings lie in rows
                    where mowers passed in the heat.
A parching scent enters the nostrils.

Morning barely breathed before
                    noon mounted on tiers of maples,
fiery and still. The eye smarts.

Moisture starts on the back of the hand.

Glass and chrome on burning cars fan out
cobwebby lightning over children
                    damp and flushed in the shade.

Over all the back yards, locusts
buzz like little sawmills in the trees,
                    or is the song ecstatic? — rising
rising until it gets tired and dies away.

Grass baking, prickling sweat, great blazing tree,
magical shadow and cicada song
                            recall
those heroes that in ancient days, reclining
on roots and hummocks, tossing pen-knives
                            delved in earth's cool underworld
and lightly squeezed the black clot from the blade.

Evening came, will come with lucid stillness
                            printed by the distinct cricket
and, far off, by the freight cars' coupling clank.

                            A warm full moon will rise
out of the mothering dust, out of the dry corn land.

                            Robert Fitzgerald

A Blessing

Just off the highway to Rochester, Minnesota,
Twilight bounds softly forth on the grass.
And the eyes of those two Indian ponies
Darken with kindness.
They have come gladly out of the willows
To welcome my friend and me.
We step over the barbed wire into the pasture
Where they have been grazing all day, alone.
They ripple tensely, they can hardly contain their happiness
That we have come.
They bow shyly as wet swans. They love each other.
There is no loneliness like theirs.
At home once more,
They begin munching the young tufts of spring in the darkness.
I would like to hold the slenderer one in my arms,
For she has walked over to me
And nuzzled my left hand.
She is black and white,
Her mane falls wild on her forehead,
And the light breeze moves me to caress her long ear

That is delicate as the skin over a girl's wrist.
Suddenly I realize
That if I stepped out of my body I would break
Into blossom.

James Wright

Finale

A Selection from "Prairie"

O prairie mother, I am one of your boys.
I have loved the prairie as a man with a heart
      shot full of pain over love.
Here I know I will hanker after nothing so much
      as one more sunrise, or a sky moon of fire
      doubled to a river moon of water.

I speak of new cities and new people.
I tell you the past is a bucket of ashes.
I tell you yesterday is a wind gone down,
        A sun dropped in the west.
I tell you there is nothing in the world
        Only an ocean of tomorrows,
        A sky of tomorrows.

I am a brother of the cornhuskers who say at
    sundown:
        Tomorrow is a day.

Carl Sandburg

I rise, I rise
I who makes the earth to rumble

I rise, I rise
I in whose thighs there is strength

I rise, I rise
I who whips his back with his tail when in a rage:

I rise, I rise
I in whose humped shoulder there is power.

I rise, I rise
I who shakes his mane when angered.

I rise, I rise
I whose horns are sharp and curved.

— Osage Chant

Of De Witt Williams on
His Way to Lincoln Cemetery

He was born in Alabama.
He was bred in Illinois.
He was nothing but a
Plain black boy.

Swing low swing low sweet sweet chariot.
Nothing but a plain black boy.

Drive him past the Pool Hall.
Drive him past the Show.
Blind within his casket,
But maybe he will know.

Down through Forty-seventh Street:
Underneath the L,
And Northwest Corner, Prairie,
That he loved so well.

Don't forget the Dance Halls —
Warwick and Savoy,
Where he picked his women, where
He drank his liquid joy.

Born in Alabama.
Bred in Illinois.
He was nothing but a
Plain black boy.

Swing low swing low sweet sweet chariot.
Nothing but a plain black boy.

Gwendolyn Brooks

Moonlight

A Selection

And in the cold, bleak winter time
When Kansas was a cheerless clime,
And ground was covered high with snow
That moonlight glittered on below,
We sat indoors and dominoes
Played or some other game; no cards
Would we play. No, like sage bards
We stuck to homely games, were foes
At checkers or some other game.
We often played the same game more
Than once — two times or three or four,
Again and yet again the same;
And still we seldom grew tired of
Those favorites, that were our love,
Outside, the icy gusts might beat;
Inside we stayed and warmed our feet.
While wind outside but whistled higher,
We stayed inside before the fire.
But those old, golden times long past,
Alas, could not forever last.

W. G. Vincent

Waldheim Cemetery

We are in Chicago's Waldheim cemetery.
I am walking with my father.
My nose, my eyes,
    left pink wrinkled oversize
       ear
My whole face is in my armpit.
We are at the stone beneath which lies
My father's mother;
There is embedded in it a pearl-shaped portrait.
I do not know this woman.
    I never saw her.
I am suddenly enraged, indignant.
I clench my fists; I would like to strike her.
My father weeps.
He is Russian; he weeps with
    conviction, sincerity, enthusiasm.
I am attentive.
I stand there listening beside him.
After a while, a little bored,
    but moved,

I decide myself to make the effort;
I have paid strict attention;
I have listened carefully.
Now, I too will attempt tears;
       they are like song,
       they are like flight.
I fail.

Robert Sward

Iowa

Air as the fuel of owls. Snow
unravels, its strings slacken. Creamed

to a pulp are those soft gongs
clouds were. The children

with minds moist as willow pile
clouds purely in their minds; thrones

throng on a bright mud strangely
shining. And here

chase a hog home as a summer sun
rambles over the ponds, and here run

under a sky ancient as America with
its journeying clouds. All their hands

are ferns and absences. Their farm homes
on their hills are strangely childlike.

Michael Dennis Browne

Old Dubuque

There is no past, present and future time
here in Dubuque, there is just Dubuque time.
                                    — Richard Bissell

        From Grant's grave Galena
        we drove down in a daze
         (from two days of antiques)
        to the Mississippi,
        then crossed over at noon
        to old, hunchbacked Dubuque:
        a never-say-die town,
        a gray, musty pawnshop,
        still doing business; while
        on the bluff, blue jeans flap
        in a river wind laced
        with fresh paint and dead carp.

        We couldn't find the house
        where she once lived and died
         (at ninety, baking bread)
        somewhere in the hard maze
        of crusty ships and streets.

And Dubuque is a spry,
goofy-sad river gal,
lost in a patchwork-haze
of tears and years gone by;
and I love this mad place
like my dead grandmother
loved her steins of Star beer.

Dave Etter

Derricks

Rolling away from Chicago
One drizzly, early morning
Aboard the Rock Island Line's
Peoria Rocket,
I saw above the grey buildings
Four bright-orange derricks
Affably nodding and deferring
To each other;
A warm, aloof, quiet conversation
Of intricate cables and steel struts.

I slid right by,
Under all that metal talk,
Leaving just two shiny rails
To mark my passing.

R. R. Cuscaden

Old Man, Phantom Dog

In late autumn the hound,
gone now ten years, has come
— or so it seems to him,
sunk in a chair at dusk —
to scratch at the back door,
its whine a faint murmur

in the cold evening. Then
his mind will shift slowly

in its old skull-bone chair
to other falls fifty,

forty, thirty years now
torn out of time: black leaves

across the stubble-field
acres where love summered,

golden-ripe. The tall boys
were that grain: lost now too,

into towns, other worlds
— as if, like her, buried.

Can he, straining deafly,
hear the hound's tail thumping

on the doorsill? It is
cold, poor thing, dead these years.

If a wife sat there now
in the dark room, if she . . .

but who can struggle up
from the old chair to let
a ghostly hound grow warm
at the unlit stove? No,

let what is buried stay
safe in its warm burrow:

farmers rest in winter
— an axiom he has.

Frederick Eckman

To Make a Prairie

To make a prairie it takes a clover and one bee,
One clover and a bee,
And revery
The revery alone will do
If bees are few.

Emily Dickinson

A Vegetable, I Will Not Be

Who would suspect, or even know
    the ivory-white innocence
    of a steaming hot cake:

Not you?
Let me tell you something.
Wheat grows a pure gold coat.
Grazing is plush green plunder.
Well,
    it ought to be splendid!
Wheat, fed on bones
    for its white flesh,
    ate gold teeth from skulls
    scattered through the yard,
        for a coat.
Green grasses:
    from green flesh at full moon.
Harvesting wheat,
    a man fell dead from heart attacks.
To the Sod!

This hot cake is moist
     and steams of three tablespoons milk —
     from a dying cow.
When time stretches me to nothing,
     read instructions of my burial carefully.
It's all taped to the bottom
     of an oatmeal box —
     third cupboard to the left as you enter the kitchen,
     bottom shelf.
It reads:
     "Lay me low in the wheat yards.

Fill my head with gold teeth.
I could not risk grassing to cows for milk;
Cows dry up sometimes.
I'd rather be a hot cake.
I will *not* be a bowl
     of peas!"

Donna Whitewing

49

An Ordinary Evening in Cleveland

I

Just so it goes — the day, the night,
what have you. There is no one on TV.
Shadows in the tube, in the street.
In the telephone, there are echoes and mumblings.
the buzz of hours falling through wires.

And hollow socks stumbling across
The ceiling send plaster dust sifting down
hourglass walls. Felix the cat has
been drawn on retinas with a pencil of light.
I wait, gray, small in my cranny,

for the cardboard tiger on the
kitchen table to snap me, shredded, from
the bowl.

II

Over the trestle go
the steel beetles, grappled tooth-to-tail over and
over and over, there, smokestacks

lung tall hawkers into the sky's
        spittoon. The street has a black tongue. Do you
            hear him, Mistress Alley, wooing
you with stones? There are phantoms in that roof's trousers;
            they kick the wind. The moon, on a
            ladder, is directing traffic
        now. You can hardly hear his whistle. The
            oculist's jeep wears horn-rimmed wind-
shields, the motor wears wires on its overhead valves.
        Grow weary, weary sad siren,

        you old whore. It's time to retire.

III

The wail of the child in the next room quails
        like a silverfish caught in a
thread. It is quiet now. The child's sigh rises to
        flap with a cormorant's grace through

        the limbo of one lamp and a
        slide-viewer in your fingers. I cannot
        get thin enough for light to shine
my color in your eyes. There is no frame but this for
        the gathering of the clan. Words

        will stale the air. Come, gather up
        our voices in the silent butler and
        pour them into the ashcan of
love. Look, my nostrils are dual flues; my ears are
        the city dump; my eyes are the

very soul of trash; my bitter
tongue tastes like gasoline in a littered
alley.

IV

The child cries again. Sounds
rise by the riverflats like smoke or mist in time's
bayou. We are sewn within seines

of our own being, thrown into
menaces floating in shadows, taken
without volition like silver
fish in an undertow down the river, down time,
and smogs of evening.

V

The child cries.

VI

Do you hear the voice made of wire?
Do you hear the child swallowed by carpets,
the alley eating the city,
rustling newsprint, in the street, begging moonlight with
a tin cup and a blindman's cane?

VII

The lamps are rheumy in these tar
avenues. Can you sense the droppings of
flesh falling between walls falling.
the burrowing of nerves in a cupboard of cans?
Can you hear the roar of the mouse?

There is nothing but the doorway
sighing; here there is nothing but the wind
swinging on its hinges, a fly
dusty with silence, and the house, on its back, buzzing
with chimneys, walking on the sky

like a blind man eating fish in an empty room.

Lewis Turco

A Siding Near Chillicothe

From the high deck of Santa Fe's El Capitan
cabs; sand-domes, stacks were seen above the box-car line:
old locomotives parked, antediluvian

in cruel progress, gone before us to that night
toward which we see, sacks of memories, slide in blander airs,
and streamline our old eyes and thoughts from glass and flight.

Our ears, boys' ears, and eyes and hearts were haunted by
huge hoots of laughter down the dark: the glow: the steam
bulging in black and red up the spark-shotten sky.

Now wheels, rails rust together, dews and sunshine eat
the iron grace: through silence their corrosion ticks
and drops in red dust, junk of grandeurs obsolete.

So, like old elephants who stumbled off to die
in their known place, and rot their bulks from ivory bones,
the locomotives stood against the prairie sky.

Richmond Lattimore

Three Kinds of Pleasures

I

Sometimes, riding in a car, in Wisconsin
Or Illinois, you notice those dark telephone poles
One by one lift themselves out of the fence line
And slowly leap on the gray sky —
And past them, the snowy fields.

II

The darkness drifts down like snow on the picked cornfields
In Wisconsin: and on these black trees
Scattered, one by one,
Through the winter fields —
We see stiff weeds and brownish stubble,
And white snow left now only in the wheeltracks of the com-
    bine.

III

It is a pleasure, also, to be driving
Toward Chicago, near dark,
And see the lights in the barns.
The bare trees more dignified than ever,
Like a fierce man on his deathbed,
And the ditches along the road half full of a private snow.

Robert Bly

Detroit

There is a cool river
which flows among the red and yellow
pennants of the gas stations,
and through the black brick
of the car factories.
Smoke does not dirty it.
Children splash through it
on their Lambrettas.
It does not disturb the drought
which burns the evergreens
on the square lawns of foremen.
Yet willows grow
from the moss on the bank.
Under the mist of the branches
sit William Blake,
Thomas Jefferson,
Huckleberry Finn,
and Henry James.
They are thinking about fish.
They are watching the river: it flows
through the city of America
without fish.

Donald Hall

Two Beers in Argyle, Wisconsin

Birds fly in the broken windows
of the hotel in Argyle.
Their wings are the cobwebs
of abandoned lead mines.

Across the street at Skelly's
the screen door bangs against the bricks
and the card games last all day.

Another beer truck comes to town,
chased by a dog on three legs.

Batman lies drunk in the weeds.

Dave Etter

Lying in a Hammock at William Duffy's Farm in Pine Island, Minnesota

Over my head, I see the bronze butterfly,
Asleep on the black trunk,
Blowing like a leaf in green shadow.
Down the ravine behind the empty house,
The cowbells follow one another
Into the distances of the afternoon.
To my right,
In a field of sunlight between two pines,
The droppings of last year's horses
Blaze into golden stones.
I lean back, as the evening darkens and comes on.
A chicken-hawk floats over, looking for home.
I have wasted my life.

James Wright

Sold

After many long months on the market,
The *For Sale* sign flaking paint,
My house is finally sold.
Poor wallflower of a buy,
No one loved you but the basement poet.
When the wind blew west
The paint factory sent my wife
Into a flurry of window-shutting;
The children somehow never found
The friends they impossibly imagined.
But my radishes prospered
In that southside, White Sox air,
And my single tree, a Cottonwood,
Ruled a forest of backyards.

Now, it is hard to recall
The sounds and passing of the
Illinois Central freight trains,
And there is no ground I can call my own.

R. R. Cuscaden

Steel Mills

Gigantic mills stand stark against the sky;
Ore freighters plow the lakes, and flats of coal
(Kentucky Elkhorn) , northward bound, pass by
The lands of early buffalo — the goal
Of each mill's ingot moulds a warship's keel,
A sword, the rails that span the nation's girth,
A piston ring, the wires that link the earth,
A plane or Pullman car of stainless steel.

Rachel Albright

Kansas Boy

This Kansas boy who never saw the sea
Walks through the young corn rippling at his knee
As sailors walk; and when the grain grows higher
Watches the dark waves leap with greener fire
Than ever oceans hold. He follows ships,
Tasting the bitter spray upon his lips,
For in his blood up-stirs the salty ghost
Of one who sailed a storm-bound English coast.
Across wide fields he hears the sea winds crying,
Shouts at the crows — and dreams of white gulls flying.

Ruth Lechlitner

Notes About the Poets

Rachel Albright. No information is available about this poet.

Sherwood Anderson (1876–1941) was born in Camden, Ohio. He is best known for his novel *Winesburg, Ohio,* but he also wrote several collections of short stories, including *Horses and Men* and *Death in the Woods.*

William Rose Benét (1886–1950) was a founder and for many years editor of the *Saturday Review of Literature.* He was the author of a number of books of poetry and in 1942 won the Pulitzer Prize for his narrative verse *The Dust Which Is God.*

Paul Southworth Bliss (b. 1899) worked as a newspaperman in Boston, New York, St. Paul, and Minneapolis, and was also a rancher in Hettinger, North Dakota. He has written nine books of poetry.

Robert Bly (b. 1926) lives on a farm near Madison, Minnesota. His books of poetry include *Silence in the Snowy Fields* and *The Light Around the Body.* He has also translated the works of a number of major Latin-American poets.

Gwendolyn Brooks (b. 1917) was born in Topeka and now lives in Chicago. She has written novels, short stories, and children's books, and in 1950 won the Pulitzer Prize for poetry. Her books of poems include *A Street in Bronzeville, Annie Allen,* and *The Bean Eaters.*

Michael Dennis Browne (b. 1940) was born in England and has taught creative writing at the University of Iowa and the University of Minnesota. His poems have appeared in numerous magazines and anthologies. He has also published a book of poetry, *The Wife of Winter*.

Victor Hernandez Cruz (b. 1949) was born in Puerto Rico. He has written two books of poetry, *Snaps* and *Mainland*.

R. R. Cuscaden (b. 1931) has lived in the Midwest all his life. From 1960 to 1965 he published and edited the magazine *Midwest*. In 1970 he became architecture critic for *The Chicago Sun-Times*. His collections of poetry include *Poem for a Ten Pound Sailfish* and *Ups & Downs of a Third Baseman*.

Emily Dickinson (1830–1886) was born in Amherst, Massachusetts, and spent most of her life as a recluse. She wrote over 1000 brief but lovely poems on such themes as nature, love, and death. Only seven appeared in print during her lifetime. The rest were discovered and published after her death.

Frederick Eckman (b. 1924) is a professor of English at Bowling Green University. His books of poetry include *The Epistemology of Loss, Running,* and *The Exiles*. He has also published *Cobras and Cockle Shells,* a book about contemporary poetry.

Dave Etter (b. 1928) lives in St. Charles, Illinois and is an editor at Northwestern University Press. His books of poetry include *Go Read the River* and *The Last Train to Prophetstown*.

Robert Fitzgerald (by 1910) is professor of rhetoric at Harvard. His books of poetry include *Spring Shade* and *In the Rose of Time*. He has also translated many poems and plays from the Greek.

Isabella Gardner (b. 1915) was associate editor of *Poetry* magazine for a number of years. Her books of poetry include *Birthdays for the Ocean, The Looking Glass,* and *West of Childhood*.

Donald Hall (b. 1928) is professor of English at the University of Michigan, Ann Arbor. He has written several books of poetry including *The Alligator Bride* and *The Yellow Room*. He has also edited a number of anthologies.

Donald Justice (b. 1925) received his Ph.D. from Iowa State University where he now teaches English. He has written several books of poetry including *The Summer Anniversaries* and *A Local Storm.*

Richmond Lattimore (b. 1906) taught Greek at Bryn Mawr College for thirty-six years. He has published many translations of Greek poetry.

Ruth Lechlitner (b. 1901) was born and educated in the Midwest but now lives in Sonoma, California. Her poetry has appeared in *The New Yorker, The Nation, The New Republic,* and other leading magazines.

John Frederick Nims (b. 1913) taught for many years at the University of Notre Dame and is currently on the faculty of the University of Florida at Gainesville. His books of poetry include *The Iron Pastoral, A Fountain in Kentucky,* and *Knowledge of the Evening.*

Ruth De Long Peterson (b. 1916) was born on a farm near Danville, Iowa. A teacher and librarian, she was for nineteen years editor of the Iowa Poetry Association's annual book of poems, *Lyrical Iowa.*

Carl Sandburg (1876–1967) began his career as a newspaperman, first in Milwaukee and later in Chicago. His many books of poetry include *Cornhuskers, Smoke and Steel,* and *Early Moon.* He is also the author of a notable biography of Abraham Lincoln.

Robert Sward (b. 1933) graduated from the University of Illinois and received an M.A. from the University of Iowa. He has taught at Connecticut College, Cornell University, and the University of Victoria in British Columbia. His books of poetry include *Uncle Dog and Other Poems, Kissing the Dancer and Other Poems,* and *Thousand-Year-Old Fiancée and Other Poems.*

Lewis Turco (b. 1934) teaches at the State University of New York College at Oswego where he directs the program in writing arts. His books of poetry include *The Inhabitant, Pocoangelini: a Fantography, and Other Poems*. He has also written *The Book of Forms and Poetry: An Introduction through Writing*.

W. G. Vincent lived for many years in Hutchinson, Kansas. His book *Poems of a Kansan* was published in 1952 but was written during the early 1930s when he was a student at the University of Kansas.

Donna Whitewing (b. 1943) was born in Nebraska and grew up there and in Oklahoma. She graduated from the Institute of American Indian Arts in Santa Fe, New Mexico.

James Wright (b. 1927) was born in Martins Ferry, Ohio and graduated from Kenyon College in Gambier, Ohio. His *Collected Poems* won the Pulitzer Prize in 1972.